Evolve:

Changing the Purpose of Business

A Short and Simple Business Guide to Social
and Environmental Responsibility

REVISED EDITION

CONNIE PILLON

evolve

evolve

evolve

Table of Contents

evolve

Introduction

This guide offers straightforward tips on how to make your business socially and environmentally responsible. Sustainable practices not only protect the planet but also benefit your business.

In addition to practicing social and environmental responsibility, companies can actively contribute to reversing the damage caused by exploitative business practices. Businesses possess the power to address significant global issues, providing entrepreneurs with a unique opportunity to become true changemakers.

The movement toward sustainability is on the rise.

Creating a sustainable future requires establishing businesses that address environmental challenges such as pollution, depletion of natural resources, the extinction crisis, deforestation, and climate change, as well as social issues like poverty, human trafficking, addiction, racism, gender inequality, and bullying.

Purpose-driven businesses have the potential to improve the world while still achieving healthy profits. Both for-profit companies and non-profit organizations can integrate social and environmental initiatives into their core operations.

It is clear that the purpose of business is evolving. Socially Responsible Investing (SRI) and sustainability have become global movements.

Changing the Purpose of Business

The primary purpose of business has been to make a profit. However, the pursuit of profit without equal consideration for people and the planet has led to overconsumption of natural resources, environmental degradation, and the violation of basic human/animal rights.

Companies that exploit people or the planet for short-term gain *(often only to produce cheap, unhealthy products that pollute the environment and offer little value)* are increasingly exposed and boycotted by today's consumers.

In addition, it is essential for companies not to misrepresent themselves as environmentally and socially responsible, which is recognized as *greenwashing*.

Business relationships should lead to win-win outcomes, benefiting everyone involved—employees, consumers, communities, leaders, investors, and the planet. This is the art of sustainability.

Purpose-driven companies can use business to evolve the world by creating products and services that integrate a social or environmental cause into their brand identity, mission/vision statements, business practices, and marketing strategies. They can also network with other companies and suppliers that share a similar business philosophy.

Despite the more primitive aspects of human nature, such as greed and exploitation, we are capable of much more, both individually and collectively. We can expand our understanding of our interconnectedness and develop a mindset of unity. Practicing empathy, ethics, mindfulness, and inclusivity offers significant benefits. Ultimately, each of us faces a choice about the world we want to create.

Purpose-driven businesses tend to have many of the following values:

Equality – Empowers team members to reach their highest potential and brings out the diverse talent within the team, treating each employee as an important piece of the puzzle.

Diversity, Equity, and Inclusion (DEI) – Employs a team of individuals diverse in race, gender identity, sexual orientation, ethnicity, religion, age, education, socioeconomic status, political beliefs, physical and intellectual abilities; provides equal opportunities while celebrating differences.

Ethics – Maintains a strong moral code that protects employees, consumers, communities, and investors.

Empathy – Actively listens to the feelings of others and builds an authentic connection to the team.

Environmental Sustainability – Manages finite resources to ensure long-term sustainability and the well-being of future generations.

Profit – Uses the triple bottom line approach, which evaluates a company's success by not only its profitability but also its impact on people and the planet.

Living Wages/Work-Life Balance – Ensures an employee's basic needs are met. Strong wages contribute to a healthy sense of dignity and a higher quality of life. Employee well-being leads to higher productivity, loyalty, and positive morale.

Community – Contributes to the needs of communities and demonstrates a genuine concern for the greater good.

Safety Policies – Implements strong safety policies and procedures to reduce risk and liability.

Transparency – Practices open and honest communication to promote trust among employees, consumers, stakeholders, investors, and communities.

Entrepreneurs have the power to build a better world. Unfortunately, many business leaders and investors still hold limiting beliefs, such as the idea that the pursuit of profit should be the sole focus of a business. This mindset is not serving the greater good, as evidenced by current circumstances.

Creating a business solely for profit, without concern for people or the planet, is a short-sighted approach. The well-being of society and the environment significantly impacts the long-term sustainability of all companies.

Even for individuals who do not recognize climate change, and the dangers associated with excess carbon dioxide emissions, there are still many compelling reasons to transition away from fossil fuels, plastic, and cancer-causing chemicals.

Now more than ever, it is important for entrepreneurs and investors to harness the power of business to solve local and global issues.

Business leaders and investors can choose to integrate social or environmental cause(s) and initiatives that they are passionate about, and which align with their products and services.

On a personal level, happiness is about feeling inspired by life[1]—and many of us spend most of our time at work. A sense of meaning and purpose helps to strengthen and empower us to face the inevitable challenges, successes, and failures of running a business. We each need to create a life that is meaningful to us personally. Creating a purpose-driven business can give us a strong sense of motivation, dedication, and determination.

---

[1] Pillon, Connie: "One Step at a Time: A Short and Simple Self-Coaching Book", Independently Published 2019

An Introduction to ESG and CSR

You will often see the acronyms ESG and CSR referenced alongside sustainability in business.

Corporate Social Responsibility (CSR) reflects an organization's commitment to practicing social and environmental responsibility. A strong CSR initiative integrated into a business's operations can demonstrate its dedication to human rights, environmental sustainability, and ethical practices.

Environmental, Social, and Corporate Governance (ESG) is a broader concept that often encompasses CSR but also focuses on measurable data and financial outcomes related to a company's social and environmental governance.

ESG has evolved from the original concept of CSR and is frequently the preferred term used by business leaders.

Why do companies need ESG/CSR?

- Socially responsible companies tend to have a positive reputation with the public and find it easier to attract quality business relationships.

- A strong focus on ESG/CSR leads to more innovative and sustainable business practices since companies are committed to continually improving their impact.

- Consumers are becoming more conscious of whether their purchases are socially and environmentally responsible.

- Companies that invest time and energy into ESG/CSR can build stronger and more authentic relationships with stakeholders.

- Studies show that employees find more meaning in working for companies that care about the greater good.

- Leaders who demonstrate a commitment to ethics and sustainability tend to influence employees to act in the same way.

- Companies that focus on social and environmental responsibility frequently experience cost savings by reducing waste and excess resource consumption, increasing efficiency, and improving risk management.

Tips on How to Create a Sustainable Business

Below is a list of general resources and tips to help you integrate ESG/CSR initiatives into your business and achieve your corporate sustainability goals:

- **B Corporation Certification**[2] is a private certification issued to businesses (including sole proprietors, small businesses, and publicly traded companies) by a global non-profit organization called B Lab. To be granted certification, companies must receive a minimum score on their social and environmental

---

[2] B Lab (n.d.): "Certified B Corporation", www.bcorporation.net, Accessed: January 21, 2020

performance. Visit www.bcorporation.net to learn more.

- **ISO Certification** helps to ensure that a company's products and services are high-quality.

  *The **ISO 14000**[3] series shows a commitment to sustainable environmental practices and helps companies to meet environmental regulations.*

  ***ISO 26000** provides detailed guidance on social responsibility to organizations of all sizes—the publication can be purchased from ISO. Visit www.iso.org to learn more.*

- **United Nations Global Compact** is the world's largest corporate sustainability initiative.

---

[3] ISO (n.d.): "ISO 14000 Family – Environmental Management", www.iso.org, Accessed: January 24, 2020

The United Nations has created 17 interconnected **Sustainable Development Goals** (SDGs) that businesses can use as a guide to help create a sustainable economy. Visit www.sdgs.un.org/goals to learn more.

- **3rd Party CSR Reporting, Certifications, and Environmental Audits** can be obtained from several sources depending on which industry you are in:

  *Reporting: External (3rd party) sustainability reporting helps a company to build validity and credibility with the public. **GRI** (Global Reporting Initiative) is an international organization that provides support for sustainability reporting. Visit www.globalreporting.org to learn more.*

__Certification__: There are many types of 3rd party sustainability certifications to choose from; it is beneficial to research which certifications are ideal for the type of industry you are in.

- **LEED** (Leadership in Energy and Environmental Design) is a green building certification program helping to make buildings and communities environmentally and socially responsible. Visit www.usgbc.org to learn more.

- **GBB Certification** (Green Business Bureau) provides assessment tools and planning to help businesses become certified as a green business. Visit www.greenbusinessbureau to learn more.

- **Create an environmental policy.** A written policy helps companies to implement a better management system to reduce environmental impact. In some industries, an environmental management policy is mandatory.

- **Create an ESG/CSR section on your company website.** Add a page about your commitment to sustainability on your website. Consumers value transparency. Be sure to state your social mission and/or sustainability plan, the ways in which you are implementing ESG/CSR, and your future goals for improvement.

- **Use government guides to (CSR) Corporate Social Responsibility and (ESG) Environmental, Social, and Corporate Governance.** Governments often provide free downloadable guides for businesses on how to implement ESG/CSR.

- **Create an internal social and environmental team.** You can set up a social/environmental team within your company through which your employees can participate and contribute ideas. The team can focus on how to improve the company's carbon footprint and social impact.

Additional Sustainability Tips:

- Measure your company's environmental impact regularly.

- Find out the unique environmental concerns in your specific region and industry.

- Share your progress on sustainable development with the public.

- Practice **green procurement** by ensuring that purchases from suppliers are environmentally responsible. Sustainable products are often less toxic and hazardous to people and the planet. Check the environmental impact of each supplier. Businesses have tremendous purchasing power and can send a message to suppliers about the importance of sustainability.

In the office:

- *Turn off lights. Make sure electronics are set to standby mode when unused.*

- *Choose reusable mugs and cups. Avoid single-use plastic.*

- *Print on both sides of paper. Go paperless whenever possible.*

- *Switch to non-toxic cleaners.*

- *Use recycled and environmentally friendly office supplies.*

- *Decorate with plants to offset CO_2 and VOCs.*

- *Use light coloured paints to make the most of natural light.*

- *Ensure plumbing and HVAC equipment are serviced and running properly.*

- *Use weather stripping to minimize heat loss.*

- *Try to find alternatives to plastic whenever possible since it is derived from fossil fuels.*

- *Reduce energy/water usage and waste.*

The Benefits of Social and Environmental Responsibility

Entrepreneurs and investors are becoming increasingly committed to CSR/ESG, Socially Responsible Investing (SRI), and sustainability initiatives. Companies that are ethical, transparent, and accountable can successfully build and maintain a culture of trust and loyalty with investors, consumers, employees, suppliers, and communities.

Employees and consumers prefer companies that have a meaningful impact on society. Many of today's business leaders are developing original and creative ways to contribute to a more positive way of doing business.

Companies that care about the greater good tend to create an inspiring work environment for everyone. Employees are more likely to be productive and make an extra effort if they know the company cares about more than just the bottom line. Most people want to make a difference—and create a better world.

Balancing social and environmental impact with a financial return is a more sustainable business approach in the long run. In today's digital age, information about a company's business practices is increasingly available to the public. Therefore, it is important that companies deliver on the promises they make. Purpose-driven businesses and those with a strong ESG/CSR program are going to stand out.

Socially and Environmentally Responsible Investing

Socially Responsible Investing (SRI) is gaining popularity. An increasing number of investors are choosing to avoid businesses known for exploiting people and harming the planet, instead opting to support companies that prioritize sustainability.

Financial and wealth management advisors are seeing an increasing number of clients who prefer purpose-driven investing, which aims to create a progressive social and environmental impact.

evolve

The trend of sustainable investing is expected to keep growing. Investors committed to purpose-driven investment strategies are seeing financial gains while achieving social and environmental returns.

The Circular Economy

In a circular economy, products and raw materials are reused, recycled, remanufactured, and refurbished to reduce waste. Circularity more closely resembles the earth's natural ecosystem of zero waste and transcends the unsustainable linear approach of take-make-waste in business.

A circular economy can help to provide a solution to the problem of natural source depletion, scarcity, and pollution.

Businesses with a circular model often rent products to consumers for a period of time as opposed to selling ownership of the goods. Consumers are then required to return the old product for recycling to receive a new product.

This can encourage a positive, long-lasting relationship between companies and consumers.

An innovative circular business model can attract investors, government grants, and funding. Circularity is viewed by global leaders as a solution to achieving climate neutrality and protecting biodiversity.

Attracting and Retaining the Right Employees

Companies striving to create a better world are more likely to inspire and motivate their employees. Naturally, employees who care about the greater good prefer to work for companies that do as well.

Here are five coaching tips to help attract and retain valuable employees:

Believe in your employees.

Focus on an employee's strengths and potential. Showing acceptance and trust increases morale, dedication, and performance.

Treat employees with the same level of importance, dignity, and respect that you would a business partner.

Create a safe space for honest, equal, and mutually respectful communication. Using an authoritarian communication style can come across as demeaning, and lead to disconnection. An empowering leadership style will encourage innovative thinking and the creative flow of ideas.

Create opportunities for advancement.

Help prevent boredom and stagnation by rewarding hard-working, competent employees with opportunities for advancement. Keeping employees in positions they have outgrown can result in them moving on from the company to seek out career growth.

Pay competitive wages and benefits. Employees are an investment.

Paying adequate wages and benefits directly impacts an employee's health, well-being, and sense of dignity.

Employees who do not earn living wages often struggle in survival mode. Poverty can cause psychological and physical harm. Quality wages will help to maintain positive employee morale.

Make work/life balance mandatory.

Burnout is a serious problem that can lead to mental and physical health issues, workplace accidents, and low productivity. Flexibility, mental health/sick days, and generous vacation time lead to higher morale and productivity in the long term. Promote wellness by encouraging employees to maintain work/life balance.

Conscious Consumers

Many consumers prefer to make purchases that reflect their personal values, effectively allowing them to "vote with their wallets." They find a sense of meaning by supporting businesses that serve as agents of positive change.

Consumers are increasingly skeptical of businesses that fail to uphold their Corporate Social Responsibility (CSR) and Environmental, Social, and Corporate Governance (ESG) commitments. Companies that neglect these initiatives face a growing risk of losing public trust and support.

evolve

It is also essential for businesses to integrate their core values with their environmental, social, and governance efforts across all aspects of their operations.

Businesses themselves are consumers as well. Companies can influence the practices of their suppliers by showing a preference for sustainable products and services.

Conscious Leadership

Business leaders have a tremendous impact on a company's Social, Environmental, and Corporate Governance. One of a leader's most essential roles is to ensure that the corporate culture is aligned with the company's **core values**. Leaders who demonstrate ethics and integrity will inevitably influence their team to do the same.

Conscious leaders practice self-awareness and model the behaviour they wish to see in others. They exercise emotional intelligence to turn negatives into positives and problems into solutions.

An effective leader knows the critical importance of making others feel valued. Leaders who actively listen to the feelings of others will foster connections and build a foundation of trust.

Leaders without ego recognize that they don't have to be the most knowledgeable in every area. Instead, they serve as the glue that binds a team of highly skilled individuals together. They create a supportive environment where the exchange of ideas is encouraged, and everyone is empowered to achieve their full potential.

Coaching Exercise to Integrate Values and Social or Environmental Initiatives into Your Business

Companies can demonstrate to the public that they walk their talk by fully infusing their core values and social/environmental initiatives into their brand, mission, vision, products and services, marketing, business practices, policies/procedures, and public relations.

There are a growing number of consulting and coaching agencies that specialize in helping companies integrate their desired social/environmental initiatives into their business.

Here is a coaching exercise designed to help you identify and incorporate your company's core values and social or environmental cause(s) and initiative(s) into your business.

__Tip__: Choosing social/environmental causes and initiatives that align with the type of business products and services you offer may lead to greater success.

1. Every business should have a list of **company core values** posted in places visible to leaders, employees, consumers, and the public. These values help to shape a company's culture and identity.

   Company core values should be updated as the vision or mission statement changes and evolves.

   If you do not currently have one, create a **list of core values** that reflect your company's deepest priorities and what it stands for (e.g., empowering team members, collaboration over competition, compassion, environmental sustainability, etc.). Each core value can be supported with a short summary. Companies usually have between three to ten values.

Research how to create a successful list of core values that sets your business apart and effectively communicates the essence of what your company is about.

2. As a brainstorming exercise, list the social and environmental causes and/or initiatives that matter to you most and that you may want to integrate into your business (e.g., poverty, homelessness, mental health awareness, animal rights, gender inequality, climate change, etc.).

   __Tip:__ It may be beneficial to focus on one major social/environmental cause that complements the type of industry you are in.

3. Review your list from step two and choose which social/environmental cause(s) and initiative(s) you would like to integrate with your social mission and/or impact statement.

   Some organizations have a separate company mission, vision, social mission, and impact statement, while others have combined them into one.

4. Brainstorm ideas on how you can actively **integrate** and **implement** your social/environmental initiative(s) from step

three into the company's mission *(purpose)*, vision *(inspiration/future goals)*, brand, products/services, business practices, and advertising/marketing strategies.

5. Create clearly defined, **measurable goals** to incorporate your social/environmental initiative(s) into your business from the brainstorming exercise in step four.

6. For each goal in step five, outline daily, weekly, monthly, or yearly **action steps** (if applicable) that you can take to achieve it.

ABOUT THE AUTHOR

Connie Pillon has a diverse educational background that includes Business-Accounting, Corporate Sustainability, Life Coaching, and the Foundations of Mindfulness.

She is a strong advocate for human rights, animal rights, and environmental sustainability. In her writing, Connie explores the benefits of incorporating life coaching, meditation, visualization, and storytelling into business and education.

She works to contribute to a new paradigm of wellness supported by empathy-driven leadership within our governing systems, recognizing and nurturing the unique emotional, mental, physical, and spiritual dimensions of every individual.

evolve

Written by Connie Pillon.
Edited using the Grammarly "Improve It" AI.